The Dog

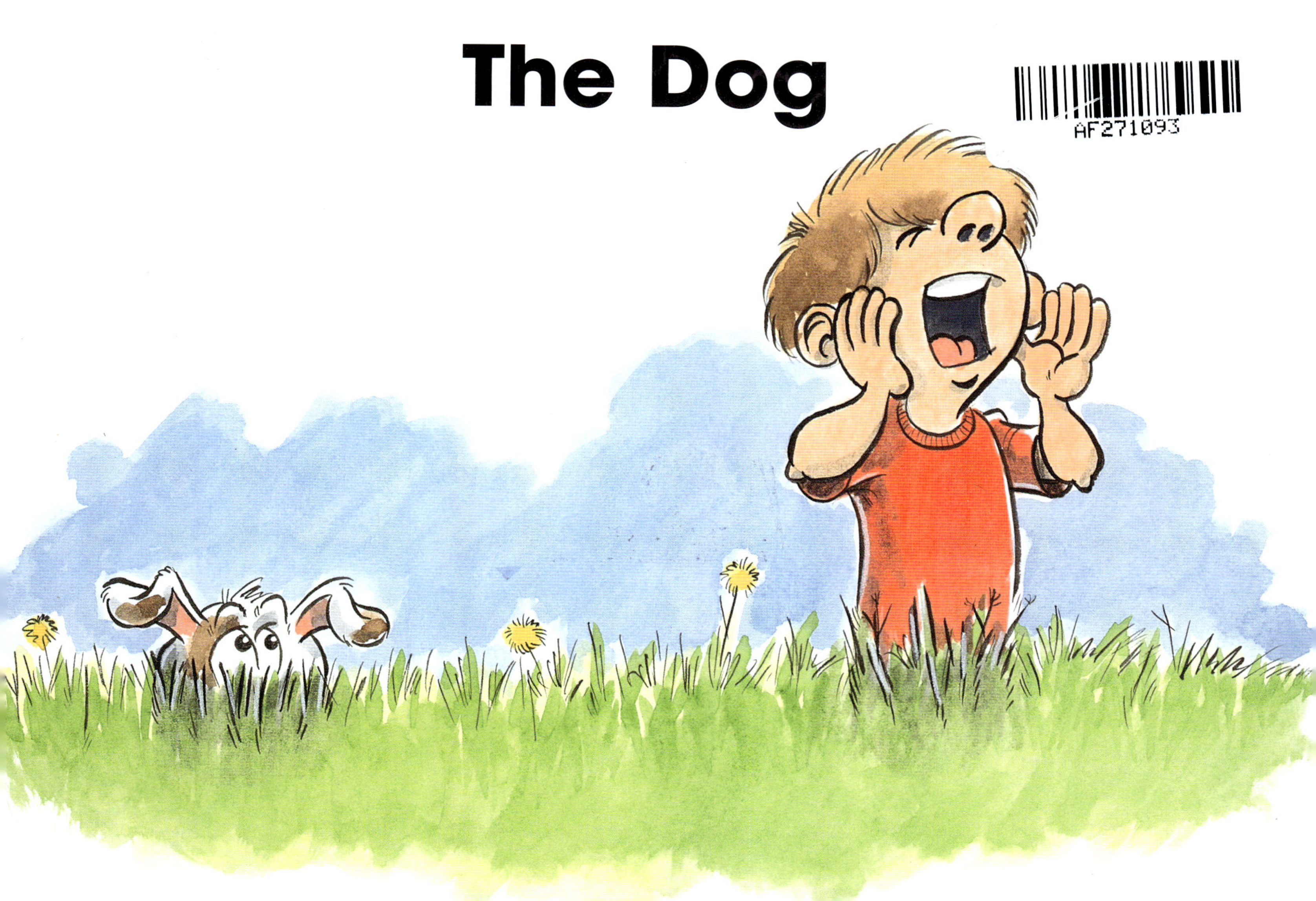

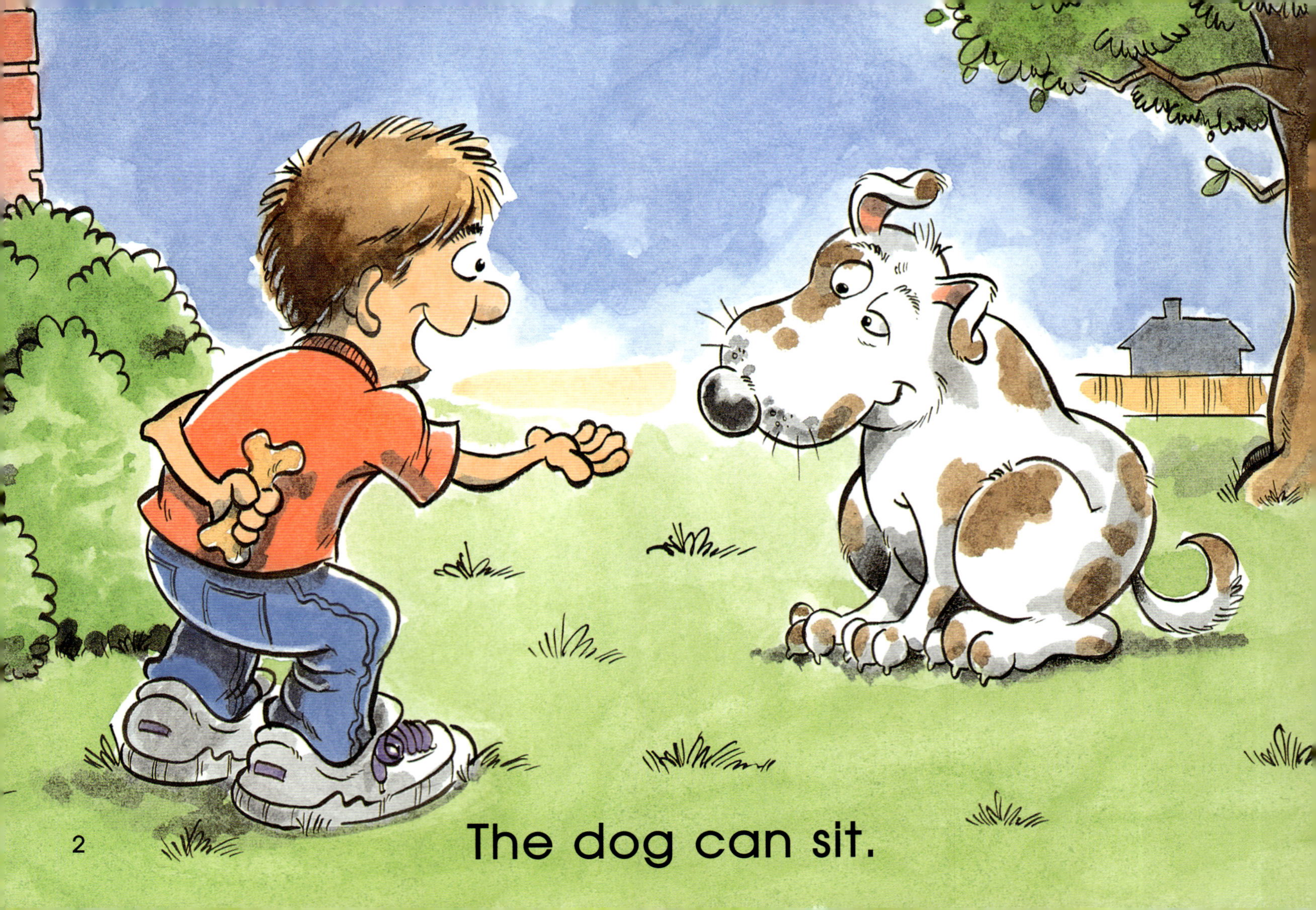

The dog can sit.

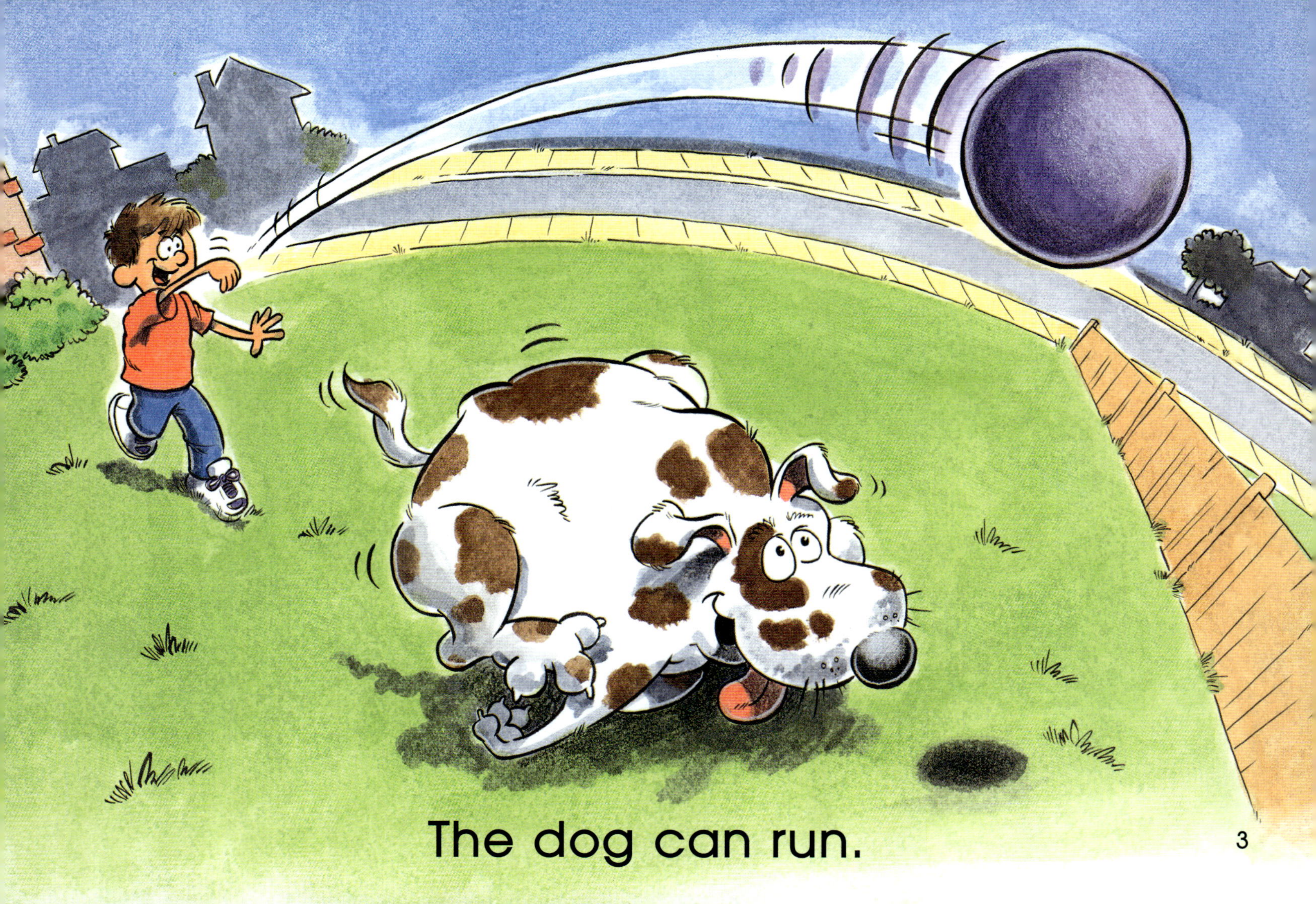

The dog can run.

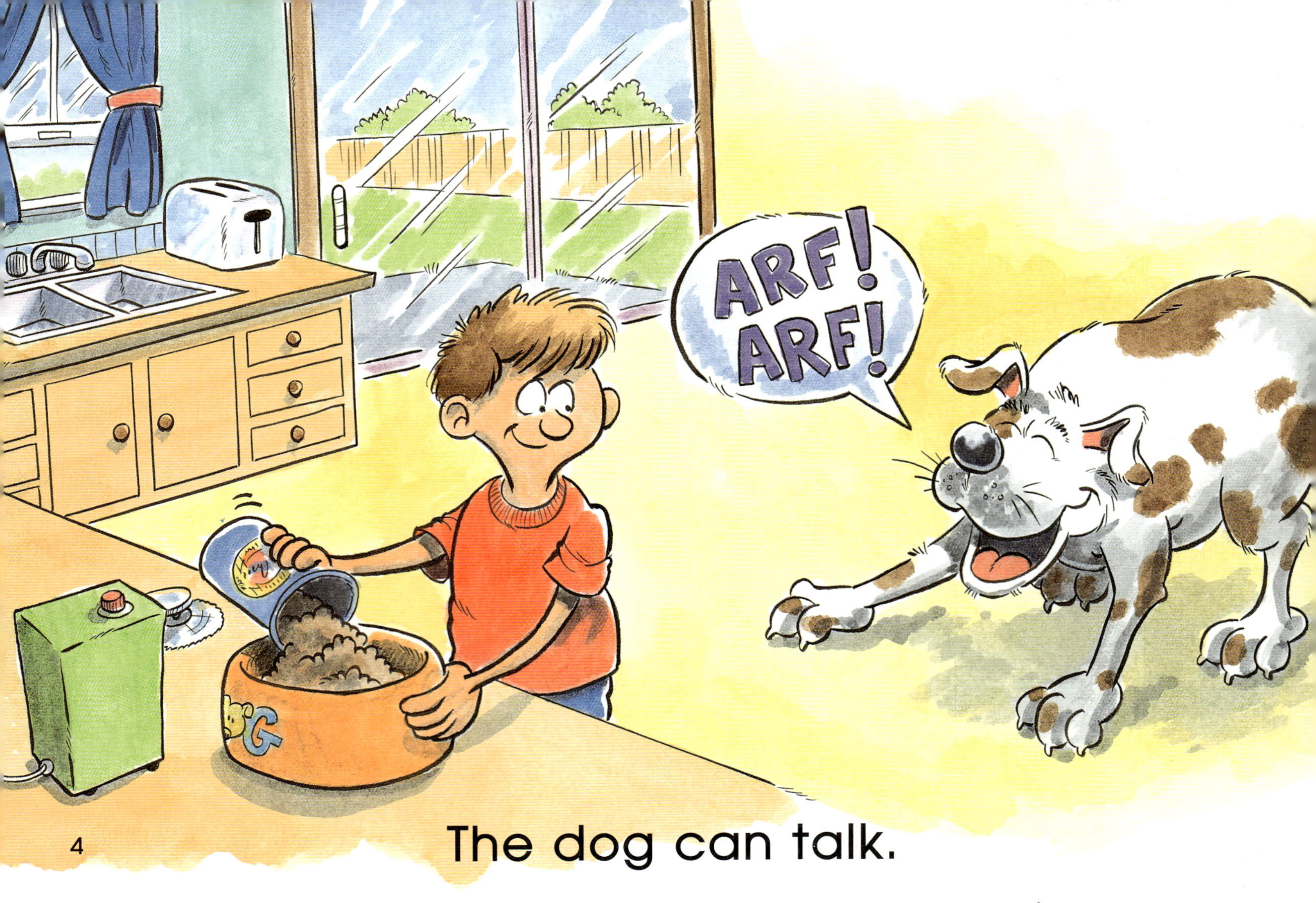

The dog can talk.

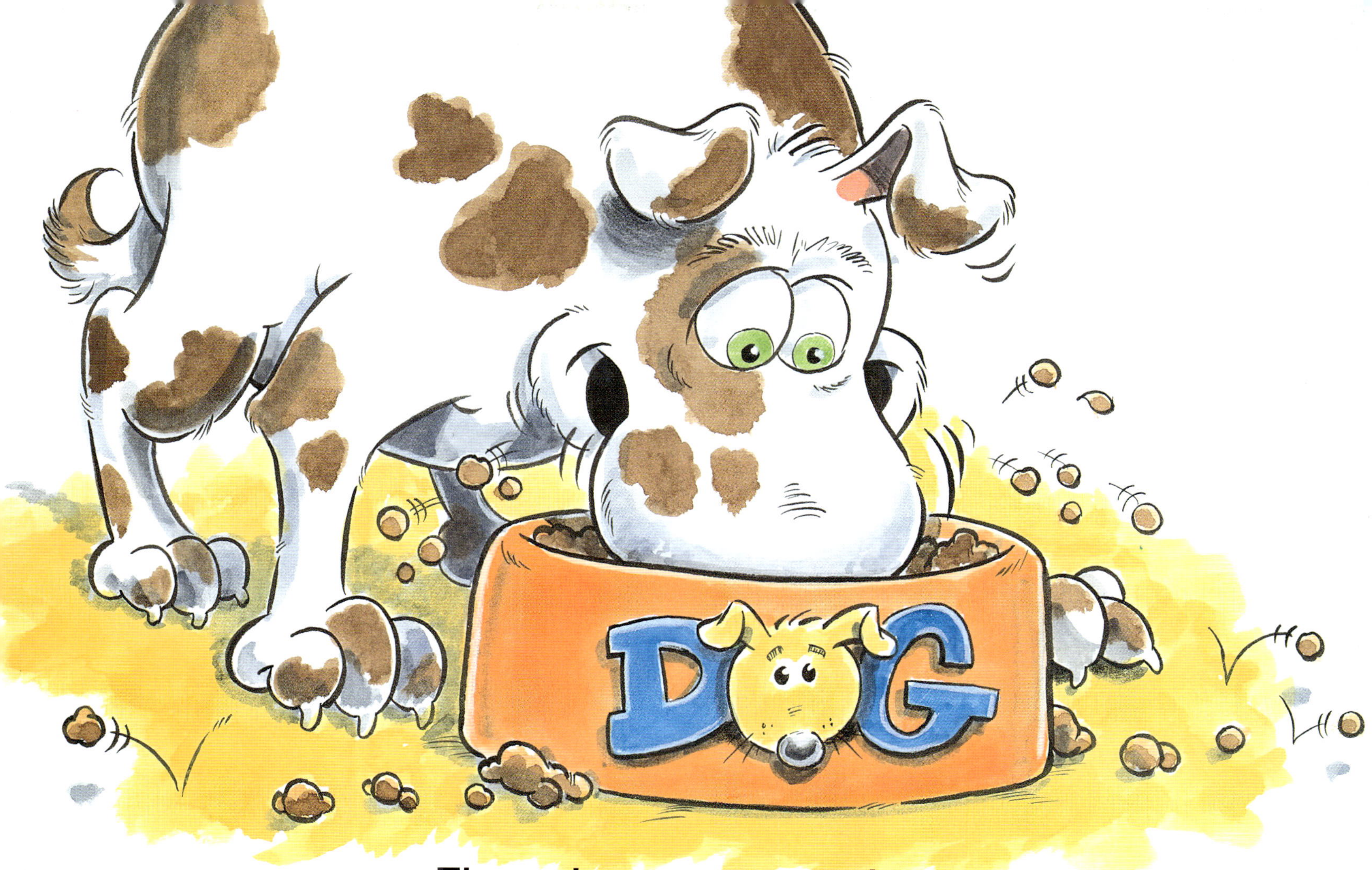

The dog can eat.

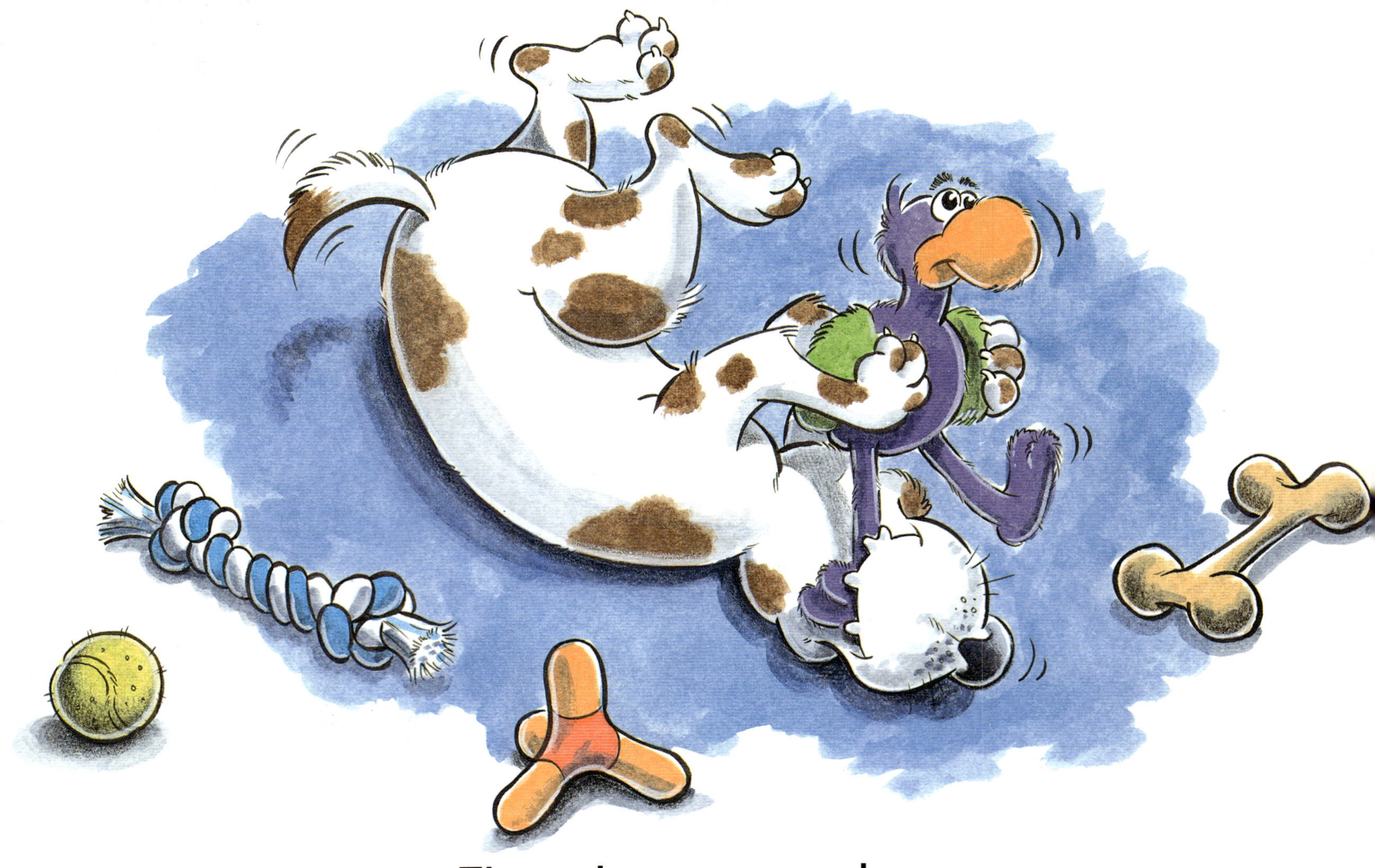

The dog can play.

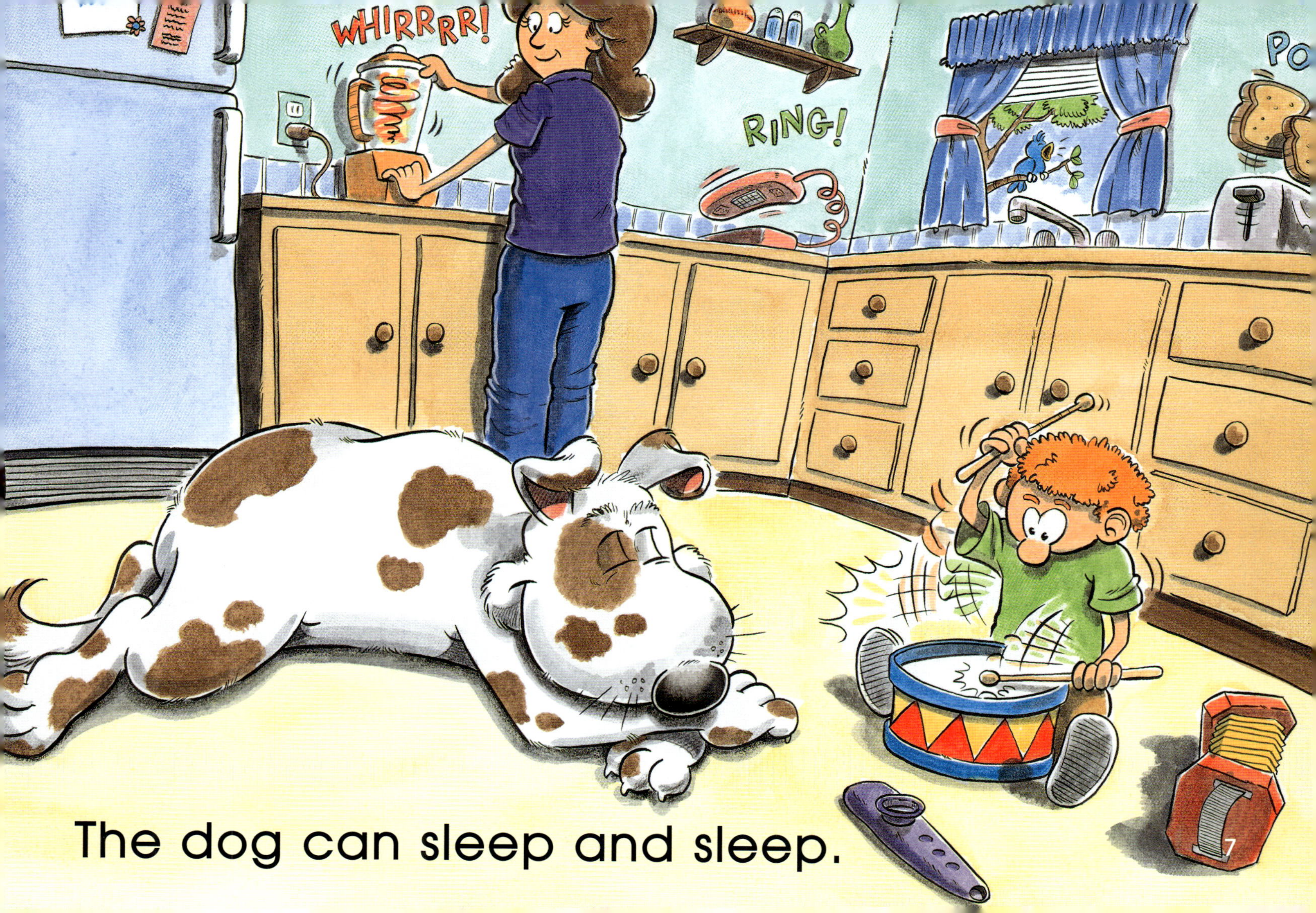

The dog can sleep and sleep.

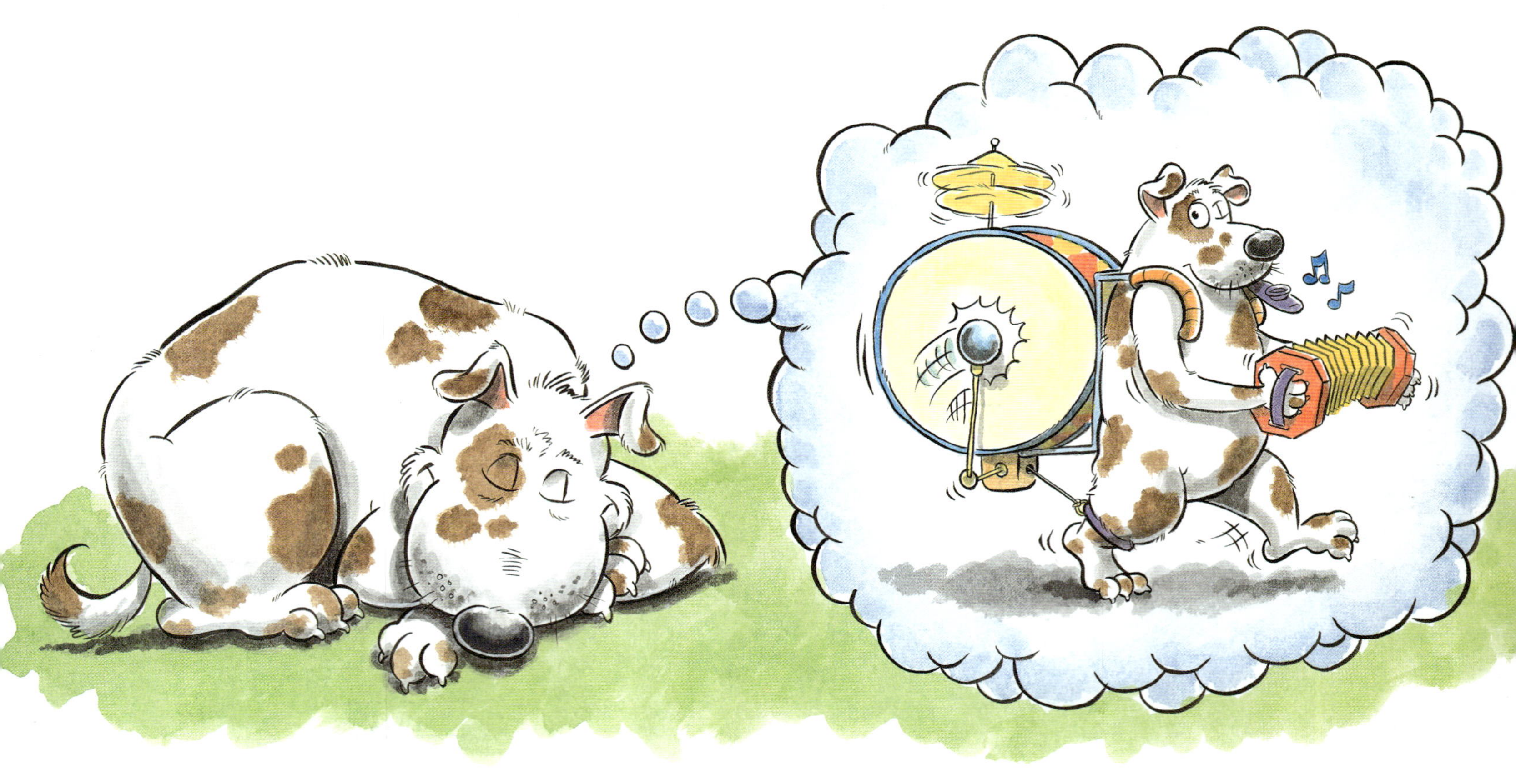

 The dog can sleep and sleep and sleep.